PLANTATION MENTALITY
1997-2015
INVOLVING RACISM NEPOTISM FAVORITISM
SEGREGATION DISCRIMINATION

by

Ruby Dee Thomas

DORRANCE
PUBLISHING CO
EST. 1920
PITTSBURGH, PENNSYLVANIA 15238

Dorrance Publishing Co
585 Alpha Drive
Suite 103
Pittsburgh, PA 15238
Visit our website at *www.dorrancebookstore.com*

ISBN: 978-1-4809-2384-3
eISBN: 978-1-4809-2913-5

CONTENTS

MY JOURNEY

JOB EXPERIENCES PRIOR TO MARYLAND COUNTY
GOVERNMENT

Job experiences, 1962 through 1998

JOB QUALIFICATIONS FOR COUNTY GOVERNMENT
VACANCIES

1997 qualifications determined by Maryland County Government

HIRED 1998 AND INFORMATION REGARDING OTH-
ERS HIRED

My 1998 hiring treatment and status of others hired/ employed
through 2002

2004 STAFF CONCERNS REGARDING TITLES/DUTIES

Staff questions job titles and assignments in Collections Section

Disregarding the binding agreement for reassignment of union members

A. 2004 & 2011 - Performance Assessment Forms (Please Note: Acting Director D.B. changed RDT's Supervisor's Rating from Outstanding to Exceeds Satisfactory in 2011;

B. 2004 - 2005 - Classifications Before Promotions for Three Clerks Although Affidavit indicated same titles - they were not- and Position #02836 remained a GC-II;

C. 1997 - 2005 - RDT's PID (Personnel Information Documents) (Please Note: Two Dates 11-27-05 and 7-10-05 indicating Promotions with no Monetary Increase);

D. 2005 - CYBORG print out of RDT's salary assignment/ changes - no PID Indicating transfers on 11-27-05 nor 07-10-05. This was apparently done upon the investigation of RTD's case filed in 2010 for retaliation;

E. 2015 - Copy of RDT's Law Suit Closure showing /S/ for the U.S. Magistrate Judge's signature which RDT believes should have required full signature; Portions of Law Suit Case - Document 27 - 9 pages; RDT's Opposition to County's Summary Judgment -13 pages without attachments; Portions of County's Deposition consisting of 10 pages;

F. 2010 - Emails from RDT's Supervisor, K.L.L. presented to Investigator SG. - H.R. Commission and J.A. - H.R. Officer which RTD believes contradicts the 2007 denials for promotional opportunities for RDT during EEOC's investigation by the Human Relations Commission in July 2010.

INTRODUCTION

This is a true story and the writer is Ruby Dee Thomas. My initials are (RDT) used throughout this story except on Pages 9-10 (RTD) is used in emails. There's need to know how people continue today to work in an environment similar to back in the day plantation-type surroundings. Initials and job titles of persons mentioned are included in every event being discussed. Think about yourself, as you read these situations that continue in a government agency today. This is the 20th century, yet you would not believe how some people's mentality can take you back to living and working during the 1960s.

My story involves racism, favoritism, nepotism, discrimination, and segregation and was brought to the attention of top officials and union representatives. Nothing and no one did anything to correct these obvious, in your face type of wrongdoings. The list of some officials aware of problems and concerns were as follows: three Directors of the Department; two or more Associate Directors; one Human Resources Officer; one Labor Relations Analyst; one Political & Legislative Coordinator; one Director of Human Resources Management; one Chief Steward Council 67 Representative and three other AFSCME Union Representatives.

The grievance that caused this situation to begin was timely filed but representatives failed to proceed through four steps necessary to complete the action. Under Article 7 A. B. - Union Security, the following is outlined: A. All employees covered by the Agreement who are members of the Union will, pursuant to paragraph B. remain members of the Union for the duration of the Agreement. All employees covered by the Agreement who elect not to become members of the Union will be required, as a condition of continued employment, to pay a monthly service fee in an amount not greater than the monthly dues paid by members of the Union, which fees will be remitted to the Union. B. The Union, upon the presentation of dues deduction authorization cards, duly executed by the individual employees covered by the Agreement, shall be entitled to have such employees' membership dues deducted from their paychecks on a biweekly basis and remitted to the Union. The Union, upon the presentation of service fee authorization by the Union to the County, shall be entitled to have such employees' service fees deducted from paychecks on a biweekly basis and remitted to the Union in accordance with the Labor Code. As you read my story, you will understand why the aforementioned was necessary to be included, for your information.

RDT's grievance was filed through AFSCME Local 2462 and as outlined above, Union members pay for representation and this process involved four steps yet, only two steps were addressed resulting in a delayed timely continuance by representatives. Top officials listed in this writing and certain supervisors depending on their grades, were not union members and had no knowledge of policies and procedures required to be adhered to by this Government Agency along with AFSCME Local 2462 pertaining to the binding Agreement. The point of interest of this Agreement in this writing is, if you don't know the rules, how or why are changes of positions and duties rewritten and in turn nothing is done when management and other personnel are proven to be wrong in the decisions they all made.

Every point written in this story involves (RDT) and other clerical staff working within the same department that allowed racism, nepotism, favoritism, discrimination and segregation to be used against many employees not only in the Department (I) worked in but, throughout the agency. Once you start reading, and understanding what (I) have gone through, it will be important because there are many others out there who may have encountered the same problems and are afraid to tell their story for fear of losing their jobs or they may know of someone faced with similar situations. (I) do not wish this type of treatment on anyone, so (I) write my story to pre-warn you.

ONE

Job Experiences Prior to MD County Government

The following outlines 36 years of experience before taking the position of Clerk-Typist I/II with the County Government in 1998. I am a double retiree and I never stopped working after the first retirement with the District Government in the year 1994. I was too young to stop working and that was the purpose of accepting the job with the County to continue in a simple job that did not require a lot of hard work as my previous job occupations had and receive benefits needed to retire a second time.

	Dates	Job Titles
Immigration & Naturalization Service	1962- 1963	File Clerk
General Services Administration	1963- 1964	Clerk Typist
US Information Agency	1964- 1967	Clerk Typist
US Department of Labor	1967- 1970	Secretary/Stenographer
Civil Rights Commission	1970- 1975	Secretary/Stenographer
Armed Forces	1975- 1977	Reservist
International Communication Agency	1975- 1979	Clerk Stenographer
Office of Financial Management	1979- 1981	Secretary Typing
Office of the Mayor of DC	1981- 1983	Administrative Aide
Department of Human Services	1983- 1994	Staff Asst./ Acting Chief-ADASA
State of Maryland (House of Delegates)	1995- 1997	Program Assistant
Board of Elections	1996- 1997	Clerk (Part-time)
PGC Office of Child Support	1997- 1998	Paralegal Assistant

Two

Status of Qualification for (RDT) -
Job Vacancies with County Government

The following outlines how (RDT) qualified for the vacancy with the County, which required testing to be placed on a register to fill the job of interest:

1. Notice to Qualified Applicant - dated May 29, 1997; Administrative Aide I/II - Rating of: Outstanding Typing examination score: 63.90; Preference of County Resident;
   Name Certified to Office of C.E. May 28, 1997; Qualification Requirement Rated Outstanding = 33; Well Qualified = 7; Qualified = 9
2. Notice to Qualified Applicant - dated July 11, 1997; Clerk Typist I/II; Written Test Score: 76.00 Preference of: County Resident; Eligible's on Register was: 24
3. Appointment to Clerk Typist I/II position was March 30, 1998; Dually allocation position upon successful completion of a six-month probationary period was acknowledged and I was non-competitively promoted September 1998 from I to II as outlined in my letter of employment.

(Review all PID (Position Information Documents) in the (REFERENCES) Section when I was employed with the County Government.

THREE

Hired 1998 and Information Regarding Others Hired

March 30, 1998, I was appointed to the position of Clerk Typist I/II in the assigned Division of the County Government with a starting salary of $18,736 and within six months upon completion of a probationary period, salary moved to $20,656 as indicated in my letter I received offering me the job. I also received a letter indicating I qualified as an Administrative Aide I/II. The office I was hired to fill the Clerk Typist I/II position, also had a vacancy for an Administrative Aide I/II. I was assigned the Typist position and a female Caucasian, was assigned the Aide position with approximately ten years or less of experience outside this Department. Well, guess what, the Clerk Typist beginning salary was less than the Aide position. So, quite naturally the interviewers, all Caucasian, would not place me in a position paying more than the person they interviewed for the Aide position. I had a total of thirty-six years' experience, thirty-two years was within the Federal and DC Government, as outlined There was a little gossip going around, you know, (hearsay), that an individual within the office where the Administrative Aide was assigned had interest in that employee but, the Aide had no interest in that person and requested to be transferred out of that office and the request was granted.

Three (3) Caucasians interviewed me (2) male and (1) female for the position of Clerk-Typist. The office I was assigned had (2) Black Clerks and (1) Black Supervisory Clerk (1) Caucasian Clerk was transferred to another office and then, all staff persons were Black. You would think the Supervisory Clerk would interview for someone coming to work under their supervision rather than have an Administrative Aide from another Division but, the Supervisory Clerk was Black—maybe they didn't think she was qualified to interview anyone. Within the next two years, one Clerk resigned and found another position outside this Agency.

There were (2) Black females hired 2000 - 2001, and both inquired about salary rates and they also had previous Government experience. After working a couple of months, both clerks became more concerned about salaries. In the presence of all clerks in that office, the Collection Supervisor, at that time stated, "The only way to receive a salary increase would be to leave, because there was no upward mobility in this office." After working approximately one year, both clerks quit, their salaries ranged $15,000 per year.

During my interview, I was advised that although I was paid $12 an hour in the Office of Child Support, I would only receive $9 an hour and after six months the salary will increase close to $11 per hour. Guess what, a female (Caucasian) was contracted in the year 2000 as a Public Service Aide-700 hours—and was paid $8.36 an hour with no experience—was hired permanently with the same job title, and was paid $10 per hour. Another (Caucasian) was hired in 2001 and was paid $11 an hour claiming she negotiated a salary because she had previously worked for a private agency. Her background only consisted of working in a hair salon and working in a nursery school. In 2006, a female (Caucasian) was hired as a contract person and was paid $10.90 per hour $22,000 per year, with no experience. She stated, "I don't like the job," and left after approximately six months. Compare my hourly salary with all the Caucasians and I had thirty-six years of prior experience but was paid $9 an hour for the first six months of employment during a probationary period and because I worked for an agency receiving monies from the County Government in a contractual position but, so did the above mentioned contractual Public Service Aide.

The Supervisory Clerk position was vacated in 2002. The position was not filled and there was a (Caucasian) Laborer wishing to become a Driver but, no vacancy was available. The Supervisory Clerk position was transferred to allow that person an opportunity to become a Driver. A (Black) female Clerk retired from this office after working fifteen years but, in the later part of the year 2004, one female (Caucasian) Clerk in this office started complaining about my title being a Clerk Typist and everybody else a Clerk I/II. Well, I informed them that I was pulled from a register of qualified tested individuals and if they wanted to qualify for the same, then they needed to take the test. They were privileged with being tested, but did not pass the test. After not being able to qualify through testing, all clerks began complaining about the type of work we all did and why we were not being paid the same salary, please note, we all did not do the same work. I was assigned different tasks than other staff persons because my skills to perform a variety of assignments didn't require an overseer and others required supervision.

FOUR

2004 Staff Concerns Regarding Title/Duties

During the year 2004, discussions amongst four clerks in that office namely, D.F. (Caucasian) stated, "If they don't pay me, I'm not going to do all that work." Neither D.F. nor J.M. did everything that (RDT) and the other Clerk, L.C. did. Clerk, L.C. (Black) closed out dates and scheduled trucks for collection pick up. No other clerk, at that time, performed that task. When Clerk L.C. retired in June 2005, the Collection Supervisor closed out dates and printed collection tickets. The Collection Supervisor assigned (RDT) Clerk Typist, with documenting time sheets, receiving tickets daily upon completion from the drivers, and entering information into the computer for weekly reports. During this time, I answered over 465 calls a day outlined in a 2004 evaluation (see refs). I was also assigned to retrieving tax information from tax records, a Supervisory responsibility, in addition to other duties as assigned and when Clerk L.C. retired, I was assigned the duties of closing out dates and truck scheduling. The other two Clerks only answered the phones, scheduled collection appointments and at the end of the day filed information. One clerk (Caucasian) in the office could not close out a day, assign trucks for pickup nor run tickets for collection without assistance. That clerk, J.M. received a six grade increase during the reclassification in 2005 and I couldn't/didn't receive a 10 percent increase in salary because OHRM management staff claimed, the position I held was already at the level they wanted everyone in the office to be. But, I qualified through testing for the Clerk Typist position and General Clerks don't require testing. I had worked seven years in this office when other clerks became concerned about my Clerk Typist title in 2004.

J.A., Human Resources Officer nor the Office of Human Resource Management (OHRM) staff, never reviewed what we all did in that office, they rewrote job descriptions based on Clerk, D.F. contact with Director, D.W. (Black Female). All 4 Clerks were requested to submit job applications along with the rewritten job description. (I) refused to sign the description approximately four times resulting in a problem with Human Resources Officer (HRO), J.A. for not responding to her request to sign and submit the job description, immediately.

FIVE

Email Requests before Reclassifications 2004 - 2005

The first email dated December 20, 2004, was sent to all four Clerks assigned to the Collection Section from J.A. (HRO). It outlined the following: "To All: As you were advised, when we met briefly last Friday, 12/17/04, the Department is moving forward with requesting an upgrade of your position. A package was prepared in August of this year -2004, requesting the reclassifications. I received a copy of the package a few weeks ago, which contains a copy of your current/existing job description and your revised/new description for the upgraded reclassification to General Clerk III. At this point, I need you to do the following in order for your package to be considered complete: 1. Submit a current County employment application, 2. Submit a current resume and 3. Sign the job descriptions (current/existing and new/revised) sent to you for your signature and your immediate supervisor's signature. I will return both job descriptions to you. Please return the signed and dated descriptions, resume and County employment application (signed and dated) to me no later than Wednesday, 12/29/04, by/before close of business. To expedite returning the job descriptions to you, I will ask (R.H. Associate Director) to drop them off to (D.M. Collection Section Head) within the next day or two for distribution to you."(Note: I refer to J.A.) (1-email on this page and 3 on page 9 are from J.A. HRO and 1 email response from RDT on page 9)

From: J.A. dated Monday, May 23, 2005 To (RTD) cc: R.H. & P.G. Subject: Signature Needed on Job Description; Importance:

High; Ms. (D.) The Department is preparing to submit Phase II of its agency reorganization. Your job description needs to be signed. R. advised that he spoke with you and you indicated you would sign it. Please contact me or come to my office so you can sign the description. I would appreciate if you would come by my office sometime on Wednesday morning as I am out of the office all day on Tuesday. Please contact me should you have questions or wish to discuss. Thank you, J.A., HRO.

From: J.A. dated <u>Friday. May 27, 2005</u> To (RTD) cc: R.H. & P.G. Subject: Signature Needed on Job Description - <u>2nd REQUEST; Importance: High</u>; Ms. (D.) Please make it a point to stop by my office sometime between Wed. 6/1 and Fri., 6/3, to sign your position description....Thank you. J.

<u>From: (RTD)</u>, dated <u>June 13, 2005</u> To J.A. Subject: RE: Signature Needed on Job Description; Sorry, but I'm just reading the email today, June 13th, we are not privilege to look at them every day. (I) did not tell Mr. H. (I) would sign this description. (I) told him the same thing (I) told you, other personnel in this office need to take the test, as (I) did. We also have one employee in our office who manages to have a title as Public Service Aide II, what about that title, will it change?

From: J.A. dated <u>June 13, 2005</u> To (RTD) Subject: Out of Office Auto Reply: Signature Needed on Job Description - I will be out of the office Mon. 6/13 - Fri. 6/17. Please contact Dr. G. regarding issues of a priority resolution to R.F. @ phone # or B.L. @ phone #of the Human Resources Office. J.A.

<u>PLEASE NOTE: THE INITIALS OF RDT SHOW RTD BECAUSE OF A NAME CHANGE.</u>

The emails listed above were submitted before promotions were approved during the reclassification of positions in the Department as discussed in previous paragraphs. From the tones of requests in these emails and the route taken to send them out for a response, there could be questions of concern. (RDT) did not respond immediately to emails as outlined, which could have resulted in management's denials and reprimands.

The Senior Clerk, L.C. (Black) had fifteen years in the Department within the same office, but retired in June 2005 releasing the Senior position as a Union member to (RDT). Since my first promotion date was effective November 2005, and L.C. had retired in June 2005, management personnel discovers (RDT) had become the union member seniority person and decided to change personnel information document to indicate the action to no longer be a promotion but, a title change. Then, another change was documented indicating that (RDT) was transferred into the position of GC-III with an opportunity for growth to apply for a GC-IV. At no time was (RDT) presented with any documentation verifying the changes in her personnel file. Apparently, no one reviewed my experiences or weren't concerned with my background as outlined in a previous paragraph.

There were (3) persons remaining in the office after L.C. retired, (2) Caucasians and (1) Black (RDT). I had a problem with my title being changed because of my qualifications through testing and the fact that other clerks did not require any testing to qualify. So, job titles were conveniently changed for the two Caucasians . This is where favoritism, racism, nepotism, discrimination, and segregation were demonstrated by the Department and (RDT) had a problem with the decisions for changes. After the so-called reclassifications, two black females were hired but, their titles were the General Clerk II and Public Service Aide held by the two promoted Caucasian Clerks. The two black clerks were never promoted to the General Clerk III titles nor was the opportunity presented. One clerk left the agency after one year and the other clerk who replaced that vacancy started working 2007 through 2012 approximately five years and never received a promotion nor title change as a General Clerk III. This was the same title one of the Caucasian Clerks held before the reclassifications in 2005. They hired personnel, after reclassifications, and the job titles the two Caucasian staff had as GC-II and Public Service Aide I/II reappeared. The two new clerks hired were Black and both had college backgrounds and they were required to perform the same duties at the lower pay level, seriously. What would you consider this act to be?

Employee rights under Personnel Law IV outlines: Employees represented under a collective bargaining agreement may be required to follow the grievance procedure outlined in the applicable Agreement. In the Agreement Article 21 - Promotions 3, such factors as knowledge, training, ability, skill, efficiency, reliability and physical fitness when equal, the employee with the greatest amount of departmental seniority will be promoted. Seniority Article 23 is defined as the length of uninterrupted service with the Employer beginning at the employee's initial hire date as a County employee. When the promotions were processed the first time, the effective date was November 2005 and (RDT) was not privileged to bargain as outlined in the Union/County Agreement. Upon receipt of a Personnel Information Document (PID) received in January 2006, the information indicating a promotion for me was incorrect and the effective date was November 2005. The salary rate prior to the promotion showed the same salary amount being paid, meaning a promotion with no monetary increase and that would not be considered a promotion. (RDT) contacted the Office of Personnel and an appointment to review the personnel folder was scheduled. There was a handwritten note in (RDT)'s file indicating a correction should be done to indicate a title change, not a promotion. In the Union Agreement previously outlined, the employee with the greatest amount of departmental seniority was (RDT) who had not reached the highest rate of pay within her grade. (RDT) had seven years two months of employment; D.F. - Clerk had four years six months of employment; and J.M. - Public Service Aide had one year six months of employment within the Collection office.

Why would OHRM Management Personnel and D.W. Director, not abide by the Agreement between Maryland County and AFSCME Local 2462? (RDT) immediately contacted W.W. AFSCME's Union Representative on January 6, 2006, and filed a grievance that was not properly processed during the year 2006. Two months after the promotions were granted to Aide, J.M. and Clerk D.F., D.F. applied for a position as General Clerk IV and had just received the promotion to a General Clerk III. How did D.F. manage to even be interviewed with less than three months experience in the lower GC-III position? Six months was required to qualify and be considered for that GC-IV. Not only did D.F. file a grievance because she did not get the GC-IV position, D.F. managed to convince officials to qualify D.F. for an Inspector position within the office where she did not get the GC-IV position. What was done to make it possible for D.F. to qualify for that job? (I) understand there was no position opened for an Inspector yet, a reassignment happened immediately for D.F..

Union Representatives and OHRM showed favoritism if compared to the request submitted by (RDT). Approximately two months or less later, D.F. received a response for the grievance she filed and race was involved, and both of us were union members. D.F. advised (RDT) of a conversation with one of the interviewers, who had passed on information regarding D.F.'s verbal score compared to the other applicant's score. Although D.F. had verbally scored higher, the applicant was already in the position but, not a union member so D.F. filed a grievance and received an immediate resolution. The applicant was a Black female contractual employee. This is where individuals working within the same Department should not be allowed to interview nor assists with hiring or denying applicants when they are not qualified Personnel Analysts. D.F. should never have been privileged to know the scores of her or the other individual. This would be known as breach of confidentiality against the individual responsible for passing on this information.

Six

2006 Grievance Filed & Union Representatives Failures

(RDT) waited ten months for Union representative J.D. to claim P.F. forgot to submit the grievance to the third step causing closure. From January 2006 through October 31, 2006, union representatives failed to carry out the four step process for the union member (RDT).

In AFSCME's Union pamphlet dated July '05 - June '07 there were fifty-one Articles involved with the Agreement between MD County Government and AFSCME and this paragraph is copied. "Article 1A - Purpose indicates: This Collective Bargaining Agreement ("Agreement") is entered into by _ _County, Maryland ("County" or "Employer") and Council 67 of the American Federation of State, County and Municipal Employees and its affiliated Locals 1170, (2462) 2735 and 3389 ("Union" or "AFSCME"), and has as its purpose the promotion of harmonious relations between the County and AFSCME; the establishment of an equitable and peaceful procedure for the resolution of differences; and includes the agreement of the parties on the standards of wages, hours, and other conditions of employment for the employees covered hereunder. 1B. indicates: Anything not covered specifically by this Agreement shall be administered in accordance with the Annotated Code of Maryland and County Personnel laws."

SEVEN

2006 EEOC Complaint Filed & Rejected

In November 2006, when (I) contacted the EEOC in Baltimore, Maryland, it was claimed three hundred days had gone by for submission of a claim for a January 2006 date of harm. A letter from EEOC was received by (RDT) dated January 2007, indicating late filing for a discrimination case and could not be processed. (I) did notify the EEOC in May 2006 upon receipt of the second documentation indicating a promotion without a monetary increase but, (I) was advised if the Union was negotiating the harm, (I) needed to wait for their closure in writing. (I) believe, if the date of harm was changed from an effective date of November 2005 backdated to July 2005 for the promotions, Please note: The effective date of the November 2005 promotion was not known to (RDT) until January 2006 and that's when the grievance was filed. The back dated July 2005 promotion change was not known by (RDT) until May 2006. At this time, I believe management personnel were having problems with me filing a grievance and were reprimanding me a second time. Not responding to emails from J.A. Human Resources Officer was the first delay problem and then (RDT) filed a grievance bringing forward a second problem with issues preventing upward mobility.

The two Clerks J.M. and D.F. received four months of back pay and (RDT) only receive a notice indicating changes. Why didn't EEOC consider the second date for filing to count as a different harm date because it became a backdated pay change and a new effective

19

promotion date. First, (RDT) was not promoted on either dates and then a change in pay is back dated four months for the other staff persons and (I) questioned the back date for the promotions. This was another penalty against (RDT) because a period of four months had passed when the position description was refused to be signed by (RDT). During this same period of time, (RDT) received a yearly merit increase in September 2005 and would have received additional pay had the promotion date remained November 2005. (RDT) was not to be privileged with the promotional opportunities, because J.A. HRO and other management staff had problems with (RDT) rejecting their requests to sign the position description that caused the delay in reclassifying the other clerks, J.M. and D.F.

PLEASE NOTE: J.A., HRO was the management person whose emails were not responded to by (RDT) on four different occasions when reclassifications for promotions were being processed in 2005.

In November 2006, (RDT) contacted EEOC and a Questionnaire was sent and responded to and dated November 17, 2006. After reviewing the questionnaire to determine whether a charge could be filed, EEOC sent a Charge of Discrimination Form 5 to (RTD) in the third week of December 2006. Since the questionnaire was received, dated and returned November 17, it was plenty of time for EEOC to send the Form 5 to consider my case timely filed. (I) have a letter from EEOC Investigator R.D. notifying J.A., HRO of the case filing. If my request for EEOC's assistance was considered late, why did EEOC Investigator send a letter to J.A. HRO notifying her of (RDT)'s submission for a case to be filed. That type of action could be considered a conflict of interest.

Under the 6th Edition Federal Laws Prohibiting Employment Discrimination, Cases interpreting Title VII outlined the following and is hereby copied. Edelman v. Lynchburg College, 122 S. Ct. 1145 (2002). The U.S. Supreme Court held that when a charge is filed with EEOC under Title VII, it need not be under oath for purposes of the limitations period. In other words, if the verified Form 5 Charge of Discrimination is filed within three hundred days of the initial unverified complaint to the EEOC, it will be deemed timely, even if the alleged discriminatory act occurred more than three hundred days earlier. Thus, even though Title VII requires a charge to be filed within three hundred days, and even though it requires a charge to be verified, it does not require that the charge be verified within three hundred days. The Court upheld an EEOC regulation permitting late verification of an otherwise timely filed charge. 142 2000e-5(b) and (e)(1)1

A letter dated December 22, 2006, was sent to RDT from R.M.D., Investigator for EEOC noting the following: "Dear Ms. Thomas: The Commission is in receipt of the intake questionnaire, dated November 17, 2006, you provided in which you allege you were treated less favorably regarding promotion and pay increase because of your race (Black) and your age (63). The EEOC is tasked with enforcing the established employment discrimination laws which include Title VII of the Civil Rights Act of 1964, as amended the Age Discrimination in Employment Act, and the Americans with Disabilities Act of 1990; however, your charge must be filed within 300 days of the date of harm. You became aware of the alleged discrimination in January 2006. Although you also indicate May 2006 as a date of harm, the evidence shows this was a continuation of efforts to address the initial harm.

It is your right to file a charge of discrimination. The Charge and any statement you provided to us will be assessed to determine what, if any, further steps will be taken in its processing, and what further EEOC resources will be devoted to its processing. If you want to file the enclosed charge against this employer, please be sure to sign and date the forms. Return the forms to the Commission at the identified address and thereafter you will receive a Notice of Right to Sue, which will provide you with the opportunity to file a lawsuit within 90 days of the day you receive the Notice of Dismissal.

Please return the completed and signed charge forms as soon as possible. Your charge is not considered filed until the forms are completed, signed, dated, and returned to the Commission. If your signed charge is not returned to us within 30 days, no further action will be taken. If you have any questions, please call me between the hours of 8:30 a.m. and 4:00 p.m. Sincerely, R.M.D., Investigator.

The above letter was responded to within the thirty days as requested and the charge form from (RDT) was dated December 26, 2006. If the charge was not timely filed, why was the following letter to the Investigator responded to by the County's Acting Director, C.W. dated January 24, 2007? It outlined the following: Re: EEOC Charge Number 532-2006-00451 - RD; Dear Ms. Ds. Investigator: This is provided in response to a complaint filed by Ruby Daniels against _County Government, Department of _. According to the complaint, Ms. Daniels indicates that she has been discriminated against on the basis of Title VII of the Civil Rights Act, as well as her age. Information provided below provides background information regarding the issue and summarizes actions taken by the Department to address the issues raised in the complaint. (Note: My previous last name was Daniels.)

(Letter from Acting Director, C. W. cont'd from above)
Background
In June 2005, the Department underwent an agency reorganization that involved the realignment of various functions and positions within certain divisions of the Department. Operations within the _ _ Division's Collection Section, where Ms. Daniels work, were reorganized. The _ _ Collection Section, comprised of five employees, is responsible for scheduling collection of _for County residents. Four of the employees occupy the position of General Clerk III, and the remaining employee has supervisory responsibility for the Section.

Prior to the reorganization an audit was conducted by the County's Office of Human Resources Management (OHRM) for the General Clerk II job classification. Findings from the audit revealed that the duties and responsibilities performed by employees who occupied that classification were more closely aligned and commensurate with the General Clerk III classification. This resulted in an upward reallocation of the General Clerk II position classification to the General Clerk III position and a 10 percent increase to the base salary of the General Clerk II employees.

At the time of the reallocation, Ms. Daniels' position was classified as a Clerk Typist II. However, findings from OHRM's audit of her position revealed that her core duties and responsibilities were essentially the same as those performed by the General Clerk III employees. Consequently, her position was reclassified from a Clerk Typist II to a General Clerk III. Since the Clerk Typist II and General Clerk III job classifications are comparably graded classifications, Ms. Daniels was not eligible for an increase in pay. Currently, Ms. Daniels is the highest paid General Clerk III in the unit. Ms. Daniels filed an official grievance against the Department requesting that the Department "make her whole" by granting a 10 percent increase to her base salary.

Department's Response
In response to the grievance, the former Department Director, D.W. met with Ms. Daniels regarding this matter and provided an explanation regarding the reallocation and the ramifications of the reallocation as it related to her pay. Specifically, Ms. Daniels was advised that the determination to reallocate her position was based on findings from an audit of her position by OHRM and that the Department did not have authority to grant a pay increase since there was no change in grade of her position.

The Department also consulted with OHRM on behalf of Ms. Daniels regarding this matter to determine if there was any other recourse that could be explored. The Department was advised that further consideration could be given to reallocating her position to a higher-graded position, which would result in an increase to her base salary. However, since findings from OHRM's audit did not warrant such a reallocation because the duties she performed were commensurate with the classification of a General Clerk III, the option of reallocating her position to a higher grade was not warranted and, therefore, not considered by the Department.

Should you have questions or require further information, please do not hesitate to contact me. I can be reached on (phone #) Sincerely, C.W. Acting Director cc: D.E.B. Director, OHRM; T.F.M.

Acting Deputy Director for E. Operations; D.H. Associate Director, W. Management Division; and J.A. Human Resources Officer.

In the above letter, corrections of information is outlined below and proof is available to show how false information was documented, but was accepted by the EEOC Investigator, because the response was from the Acting Director of the Department, C.W. with no questions asked and all information was approved right or wrong regarding (RDT).

Under Background, and the letter above from C.W. Acting Director, it was documented and show five employees, there were only four employees and the Supervisory Clerk position no longer existed; the four employees before the reorganization had different titles than outlined: (RDT) was a Clerk Typist, J.M. was a Public Service Aide; D.F. was a Clerk II; L.C. was a Clerk II before the promotions in 2005. C.W. Acting Director, stated, "An audit was conducted," to my knowledge no audit was ever performed, the job applications were requested from each individual clerk and then presented to J.A., HRO, and that information was utilized to compare job duties. Outgoing Director D.W. never met and advised me of any ramifications regarding my salary, a letter was written to me advising that the grievance I filed was directed to the wrong department and it needed to be resent to the Office of Human Resources Management and not through DER. The following letter has been retyped outlining what Director, D.W. actually wrote to me and no meeting was conducted as stated by Acting Director, C.W. The letter was dated February 13, 2006, and addressed to: Ms. R.T. Daniels, Riverdale, Maryland 20737. Re: Official Grievance -Merit Increase— Dear Ms. Daniels, I have reviewed your grievance and determined that the violation cited, Article 21, Section A, of the Collective Bargaining Agreement between County and AFSCME, Local 3279, does not fall within the purview of the Department of__. J.A. HRO, advised you of this Information during a meeting held on January 18, 2006, and suggested that you direct your grievance to the County's Office of Human Resources Management (OHRM). Should you have questions or wish to discuss this matter further, please contact J.A. HRO, at ___. Sincerely, D.W.

Director cc: to Director, OHRM; T.M. Acting Deputy Director for E.O.; J.D. Chief Steward, AFSCME, Council 67; J.A. HRO; Departmental File.

EIGHT

2006 - 07 Emails Regarding Reopening of Grievance

In January 2007, I contacted Political and Legislative Coordinator, S.P. to seek reopening my grievance, since the representatives had delayed my January 2006 filing. The Coordinator sent an email to W.H. — Labor Relations Analyst- Office of Human Resources requesting a meeting to resolve the issues. In an email from W.H. it was stated, "When it came to my - (RDT) promotional opportunity, it was a typographical error, it was not a promotion, the request would allow for career growth to a General Clerk IV." If W.H.- LRA, had reviewed my background, he would not have written such a statement. Why would (I) need career growth, with thirty-six years of Federal, D.C. and the State of Maryland Government experience with titles of Administrative Aide, Staff Assistant, Paralegal Assistant; (I) can go on naming my qualified titles. W.H. could only be making that statement for inexperience candidates — the two Caucasians — who received a promotion and title change. (I) did not need career growth, when (I) was hired to work in that office, (I) was over-qualified and seven years two months of additional experience was added to my qualifications at the time of the reallocation. Since Union Representatives had not carried out my grievance from January 2006 through September 2006, I contacted, Ms. S.L. on September 18, 2006 and was put in contact with the Acting Representative, S.P. and emails were submitted from him to the following individuals and no resolution to his request was acknowledged either. The outlined retyped emails were as follows: To: Ruby T. Daniels From: S.P. cc: B.S. Subject: Re: Meeting Dated: October 27, 2006: Hello Ruby: The email for B.S. and her cell phone in Baltimore is: a number was noted and the message was: I am sure she will call you quickly. Please let me know what I can do to be of assistance. sdp

To: S.P. : Re: Meeting From: Ruby T. Daniels Dated: October 26, 2006 Re: Meeting

Thank you S. for all you've done and I wish you could remain the rep. Is there an email address or phone number for B.S., just in case she can't get in touch with me. Thank you again. To: Ruby T. Daniels From: S.P. cc: afscme@msn.com Subject: Meeting ruby: I still plan to make sure your grievance is reinstated as well.. your new rep, B.S. will be calling you to make sure it gets scheduled, sdp To: S.P. From: W.B.H. cc: J.D.; J.A.; T.B.; K.G.-J. Subject: Meeting S. On Ms. Daniels case, I've explained to J. the Agency Reorganizational Plan (ARP) where Ms. Daniels was reclassified from a Clerk Typist II (C10) to General Clerk III (C10) (now A scale) was requested to allow for additional career growth. The GC III classification has a IV (C12) level for which Ms. Daniels can make application whereas the Clerk Typist ends at the II level. The PID (Personnel Identification Document) J. showed me contained a typographical entry error, which indicated that the action was a promotion. It was not. We would be happy to meet informally on a "get to know you basis" with the Council's new bargaining team and our new team sometime next week. Let me know a couple dates so we can set it up. Thanks. B.

From: S.P. Date: Monday, October 16, 2006. To: W.B.H. cc: afscme@msn.com; Daniels, Ruby T. Subject: Meeting B.: It is my understanding you have material showing that a grievance was begun for Ruby Daniels. J., Ruby and I would like a chance to sit with you informally and see if we can find a solution. Do you have time this week? Thanks S.P. Political and Legislative Coordinator, AFSCME Council 67 cell: ___. Please note: All the above emails were submitted before contact with EEOC and as you read, no meeting was ever conducted to try to resolve the problems I was having with OHR management staff and union representatives. Since my issues were continuing with no resolutions during that time I had to contact someone outside to assist me with my unresolved issues.

NINE

2006-07 Padding the Office with Supervisory Personnel

An Administrative Assistant (Caucasian) female was assigned around the latter part of December 2005 to the Collection office as a Supervisor and had never supervised anyone before. She did not know anything about the Collection Section but, was assigned to oversee the operation. She requested that I train her on how the office operates and also discussed why she had been sent there. She advised me that, she used too much leave taking care of an ill family member and believed she had been sent to this office as punishment. She retired around September 2006. Immediately after she retired, another (Caucasian) female was padded into the Collection Office as an Administrative Assistant and both were paid high salaries compared to the salary paid to the Black Supervisory Clerk. Although there was no vacancy in that office for the Supervisory Clerk position, they managed to put (Caucasian) employees in this office regardless of what their salaries were. Compared to the Black Supervisor whose salary ranged approximately $39,000 yet, the females (Caucasian) were paid $72,000 and up. What would you call that?

I was assigned to all kinds of work assistance situations but, no one arranged an increase for me, but I managed to train everyone who came to this office and only received due merit and cost of living increases as scheduled. People who came to work, as I did, were not privileged to receive upward mobility. If you did not come to work, you manage to move right on up the ladder with no problem. I managed to run the office without any designated Supervisor when the Supervisory Clerk left in 2002. Did I receive any incentive for my hard work and training? NO.

When the second (Caucasian) female reported to work in the office, she did not know anything regarding the operation of Collections either. This supervisor recognized my knowledge and abilities and started submitting requests for me to be promoted to a General Clerk IV within four months of her tenure but, the requests just disappeared. Management staff personnel were retaliating against me from the day I refused to sign the position description in 2005 throughout the year 2007. The Supervisor, K.L.Administrative Assistant submitted three requests to promote RDT to a General Clerk IV and none of the requests were acknowledged throughout the year 2007. The requests disappeared, claimed never received by management staff and Union representatives were constantly being contacted regarding failures by all.

The Collection Supervisor from 1998 throughout 2004, managed to remain at the landfill over fifteen years, and brags about a six figure salary for doing nothing. Yet, he told all Black females under his supervision in the Collections section, "You will need to leave this office to make more money." Why is he still there?" This Supervisor continued to move right on up the salary scale along with another coworker male, (Caucasian) who worked as Assistant Collections Supervisor before the reorganization in the Collections Section. There were quite a number of family members working together in that Department and managed to receive jobs when they claimed there were budget constraints. Caucasians manage to manipulate the system and advance, yet when it came to Black employees no chance for advancement was possible. Why?

TEN

2009 - 2010 Discussions Regarding Furloughs

Furloughs began August 2, 2009 through May 8, 2010, and eighty hours of leave without pay was initiated and compensation was reduced. This is the only time there was notification of budget constraints which would have been a concern that no one could/would be promoted or hired. This was understood but, my charge of discrimination regarding retaliation didn't get filed until June 2010. All employees were required to use all their furlough leave during the twenty furlough pay periods at four hours a pay period. The savings the County should have received, during this period, should have privileged results that would not cause any budget constraints. My attorney requested information regarding personnel promotions and hiring and the following information was submitted:

LAST /FIRST NAME	ACTION	DATE	CLASS	POS#
NOT REVEALED	PROMOTION	1/4/2009	ADMINSTRATIVE	01573
	NEW HIRE	2/2/2009	RCI VII	01785
	PROMOTION	2/2/2009	PSI IV	02473
	NEW HIRE	3/2/2009	ENGINEERING TECH IV	06780
	NEW HIRE	3/2/2009	PUBLIC SAFETY AIDE I	02956
	NEW HIRE	6/22/2009	ENGINEER VII	07203

The month of July, every year, is when budget changes occur. During requests for documentation, my attorney acquired the above information. The retaliation case was filed in June 2010. All of a sudden, no promotional upward mobility for the next year or was it just coincidental for the new budget not to include 2010 advancements for employees. Furloughs were ending in May 2010 and if all employees fulfilled the required leave without pay request, there should have been plenty of money back in the budget to fulfill any pay increases, If you assume the above information was true, they promoted two employees in January and February 2009 and, hired four new employees in February, March, and June 2009, please note, furloughs began August 2009. Apparently, there was a problem in the budget office, someone or a number of personnel were out of control for not being able to properly manage the budget and see the deficiency and no new hiring nor promotions should have been approved during that time period. There were a couple of employees, that I am aware of, with relatives in offices that could be considered to have been privileged with special treatment and this type of action would involve nepotism and favoritism.

My supervisor started submitting requests to promote me again, to a GC-IV in April 2010 and I was not aware of the problems with the budget until an investigation was underway and reassignment was being requested for me. The charge filed in June 2010 related to continuous retaliation by management with no possibilities for any advancement for (RDT). The management staff knew the only way to try to clear the records regarding no promotional opportunities for me was to use, Budget Constraints.

ELEVEN

2010 - 2012 Reassignment, Failure to Abide
By Union Agreement, and Preferential Treatment

RDT was reassigned in June 2010 with no monetary increase and remained in that position thirteen months—my title remained General Clerk III yet, I performed duties of an Administrative Aide a higher paid salary should have been initiated. It was not. In June 2011, there was a meeting with my Supervisor, K.L. and the Crew Supervisor, W.W. that I had been assisting for thirteen months and there was a shortage of staff in the same Section I had been moved from. They wanted me to assist that Office until a staff person return to work from maternity leave and to also continue working in the other position. I told them NO, I will perform only one position and since there was no monetary increase, I requested to work in the office with the shortage of staff, under the same Supervisor, K.L. because I was not going to be used anymore and especially since no money was being offered as outlined in the Union Agreement.

The following retyped email was submitted: Date: June 25, 2010; To: K.L.-Admin. Asst.; (RDT); A. A.-W.; cc: C.A.A. Associate Director; From: V.L. Subject: RE: Collection Changes; Importance: High All, As indicated in prior discussions, this effort is to relieve administrative duties once assigned to the Collection Operation's Administrative Assistant - Ms. K.M. and currently performed by W.; C.; and K.L. Ms. Thomas will be assigned to the Collection Operations Unit effective Monday, June 28, 2010. As such, Ms. Thomas will perform administrative duties of the Unit to ensure quality customer service. In addition, Ms. Thomas will eventually be assigned all administrative tasks, included and not limited to processing employees' time, tickets, scheduling, and tasks associated with Collection Operations Unit. It is my expectation that Ms. Thomas will assist the Collection Call Center (answering telephones and other tasks) as needed and during lunch. Ms. L. will coordinate the Collection Call Center needs with Ms. Thomas. More importantly, at this time, Ms. Thomas will continue to be supervised by Ms. L.

Second email: Date: June 25, 2010; To V.L. Collection Section Head; A.A.-W.; From: K.L. Admin. Asst.; Subject: Collection Changes; I am having the computer and phone moved for Ruby Thomas in order for her to assist W.W. and C.W. However, with C. out already under doctor's orders, and once she has the baby will be out for another two months, and with Ruby Thomas moving to help the Supervisors, I am proposing the following in order for the Collection Call Center to maintain functionally and continue to provide excellent customer service to the constituents that either call in to the Call Center or e-mail for Collection requests. The Collection Call Center is virtually going from five Call Agents to three Call Agents. 1. Until C.B. returns from maternity Ruby Thomas will assist in answering the phones between noon and 1:00 p.m. on a daily basis. (This has already been discussed and agreed upon). 2. I will be able to ask Ruby for her assistance when we are short staffed. (This has already been discussed and agreed upon.) 3. In April, May and June, every Monday, we have received more than seven hundred calls with a couple of Mondays receiving eight hundred or more calls. Along with the phone calls on Mondays, emails received have been seventy or more. I would propose to have Ruby Thomas stay assigned to the Collection Call Center on Mondays, and have her assist W. and C. Tuesday through Thursday until C.B. returns. Your consideration and approval will be greatly appreciated. Once decided I will inform Ruby. Thank you.

The above emails were retyped and do not reveal complete identity of the senders but, all information has been typed in exact form with exception of the full name of the office. (RDT) was assigned to perform duties of a higher job classification, but was not compensated as outlined in Article 18A. Temporary Assignments. A. Employees who are required to perform duties of a higher job classification after one (1) workday shall be compensated retroactively at the rate of that higher classification. No employee shall be required to perform such work for more than one hundred twenty (120) days in any one (1) calendar year. The employee shall receive a performance assessment if they remain in the higher classification for more than (30) days. Employees(s) detailed to a position shall be given consideration should they make application once the position is announced. (RDT) performed the assigned duties without the pay increase for thirteen months and this would be a violation of the binding Agreement that was not even considered by any management personnel nor Union Representatives and they were all aware of these actions against me. The negotiated Agreement between the County Government and AFSCME Local 2462 did not privileged (RDT) as a union member with the right to bargain collectively subject to the terms and conditions i.e., transferring union members outside current classification and becoming a non-member; failing to follow binding agreement when duties at a higher position exceeding 1-120 days was not paid at the higher grade level rate; union representatives failure to continue processing my grievance Steps 2 through 4 causing the union member to seek outside assistance in the middle of November 2006 with (EEOC). Yet, it was so convenient for other clerical staff to be promoted and continue previous work assignments.

TWELVE

Incidents You Won't Believe Happened

In June 2010, when I was assigned to assist the Crew Supervisor, I asked if a wall and door could be built around the assigned area and I was told, NO money was in the budget for that to happen. Yet, around August, a female (Caucasian) was sent from the Office of the Director to work and assist the Crew Supervisor that I had previously assisted. The Director had visited the area where the individual was being reassigned and when that individual arrived to perform new responsibilities, guess what happened?

The area where I and another Black female had to seat was remodeled/shut down and that individual was moved into the Crew Supervisor's Office and he and his assistant were moved out to the other side of the building so this individual would be comfortable and without all the noisy surroundings. Would you call this - preferential treatment, privilege character, favoritism, remember what I mentioned above - the Director visited the building before this person reported to work in the area. So, would you think he authorized the change for this individual but, not for anyone else? After working approximately three to four months in that position, this person was not satisfied, and was conveniently reassigned to work in a location in a different building within the same area. Where did this position come from?

During the same time, I continued to be denied a promotion due to budget problems, a building for the new reorganization of staff being relocated to this location was done. Personnel was brought in to occupy this new location from the Office of the Director and other offices and the salaries for some was outrageous, especially when you visit the area, normally either no one is in the new building or the personnel in the building was doing absolutely nothing. There were several staff assigned to this location and were paid Six Figure Salaries and had no knowledge of duties they had acquired and I know this because when you had questions pertaining to the operation, they could not respond but, you are being paid these big salaries. I had a problem with the continuous pay out for non-workers and personnel actually working cannot get paid properly for work being done yet, they continue to pay unknowledgeable personnel.

In 2012, there was an advertisement for non-union G-Scale volunteers to work in a newly established Call Center (311). There were four staff persons in the Office I worked in and (two persons volunteered) and two did not. The two volunteers went for training two days and were totally dissatisfied and returned to the Office where they were originally assigned. The next day after they returned to the office, the other two staff persons were advised of a meeting and letters were given to all four to report to the 311 Call Center and a date was given for reporting. I asked the Associate Director in front of the Director and a Union Representative at that time, if I could remain and work with the Crew Supervisor until I retire and I was told, No, I could not. It was claimed, RB, County Executive initiated this request. I only had six months left before I would have had fifteen years of employment with this Department and could have retired with the age and years of service for full benefit. I did not want that Call Center position because the salary would not have remained and other benefits would have caused an inconvenience plus, although the Union failed me, the privileges that were provided being a member would have been dismissed. I retired October 31, 2012, and I consider this action a force out. The fourteen years six months in the same department although, I was never promoted, would have wiped me out as the Senior union member.

THIRTEEN

2013 - 2015 Lawsuit Filing and Court Conclusions

January 30, 2013, RDT filed a lawsuit against a Maryland County Government Agency and was never privileged to present any evidence to a court of law. Yet, the Defendant's defense attorneys, two years later, are granted Motion for Summary Judgment and all Plaintiff Ruby D. Thomas evidence and opposition is just dismissed and disregarded. I filed the retaliation case in June 2010 and it took Human Relations Commission from 2010 until 2012 to consider investigating the charge, no concerns regarding the long period of time they were privileged with and no limitation for wait time. Once the Commission finalized their investigation in 2012 with assistance through EEOC, and manipulating evidence, an additional two years were wasted for the determination decided for a lawsuit to be filed. The EEOC decided with the Human Relations Commission and the lawsuit filed in January 2013 wasted another two years only to have the case closed due to budget constraints decided by a Magistrate Judge on January 23, 2015. They wonder why people are provoked. Seriously. THE BUDGET: From the time requests were being submitted for a promotion in the Department I was assigned, over nineteen employees either retired, died, or just left. This is a count of Personnel (I) knew about. What happened with the budget where all of these positions received pay from? Although some positions were filled, they were not filled immediately. There was a period of time when furloughs were effective from 2009 through 2010 and there may have been budget concerns then. Yet, during the time for upward mobility for one individual 10 percent could not be granted. Retaliation began from 2004 throughout time involved for the same individual, (RDT), with no chance for advancement. I have copies of all Organizational Charts outlining every position filled for the year 2005 and 2010 verifying changes in salaries for all employees during the so-called budget constraints that was supposedly preventing a promotion for (RDT). I should have protested my case being dismissed in front of the Court where that Judge responsible for not having a pre-trial for me and agreeing with every document submitted by the defendant's defense lawyers. So listen up everybody with a problem as presented in this story, tweet your problem(s), or protest your case in front of a court better still, write your story in book form.

In 2013, my attorney became incapacitated and I became Pro se _ without an attorney. The lawsuit had been filed in 2013 with the Federal District Court of Maryland and a Judge had asked if I wished to continue the case as pro se and I chose to continue without an attorney. Please understand, a retainer was paid and I couldn't afford to pay another retainer and the case may or may not have resulted in the same manner. When my attorney became incapacitated, he passed the case on to another attorney, who accepted the case upon request from that attorney, but he later rejected the case. There were hundreds of documents put together for this case and I am totally dissatisfied with the outcome. This case never received the proper closure according to the supposedly law and I did not receive JUSTICE. I believe because of whom I was filing the case against—Maryland County Government— individuals were paid to submit false information and make the problem go away. I had every right to be heard in a court of law before a Judge or Jury. I was not even privileged to a pre-trial. This case should not have been DISMISSED without proper closure because falsified information was presented by the defense team for the County Government. If I could have presented my evidence, I guarantee I would have had a chance to prevent anybody else from going through the racism, nepotism, favoritism, discrimination, and segregation that I underwent while working in this County Government Agency.

The Judge didn't even take time to write a full signature upon closing my case in favor of the defendant, an /S/ was in place of a signature, anybody could have reviewed and entered that. If a case was being reviewed and it took two years to finalize the case and then never go before a judge, jury, nor a pre-trial, someone should have made sure a full signature should have be documented on the letter of closure. I am full of disgust with this Court and the County Government getting away with this injustice. I would hope someone with a TV talk show would allow me to discuss this situation and maybe create a movie behind all of this. For certain reasons the case could not be heard in an Appeal Court and the Supreme Court required an attorney to represent you and the cost was $300 for Supreme Court and $500 for the Appeal Court. I'd rather write this book and take a chance on all this information being presented to the public in writing than spend money and maybe receiving the same results, I'll never know. No one, out there, should go through this type of situation wasting time, energy and effort as I did for absolutely NOTHING. Write a book, try to get the Media to listen or today, tweet your concerns, you would get more attention to the situation.

This was the worse job I've ever had and I have worked in many locations. It was set up with three one-level buildings—looking just like a PLANTATION from back in the early 60s. Believe it or not, if some of the SO-CALLED Supervisors could have a whip, they would have tried to use it. WHY is this Government Agency allowed to operate this way and when someone try to report the situation, no one is listening or they are listening but, just not doing anything about it. I would never refer anyone to work at this location as long as it continues to operate the way it is. The MENTALITY—at this location— the minds are just not working for some or they are ALLOWED TO operate one way.

REFERENCES

A. 2004 & 2011Performance Assessment Forms (Please Note: Acting Director D.B. changed RDT's Supervisor's Rating from Outstanding to Exceeds Satisfactory in 2011;

B. 2004-2005 Classifications Before Promotions for Three Clerks Although Affidavit indicated same titles—they were not—and Position #02836 remained a GC-II;

C 1997-2005 RDT's PID (Personnel Information Documents) (Please Note: Two Dates 11-27-05 and 7-10-05 indicating Promotions with no Monetary Increase);

D. 2005 Cyborg print out of RDT's salary assignment/changes—no PID Indicating transfers on 11-27-05 nor 07-10-05. This was apparently done upon the investigation of RTD's case filed in 2010 for retaliation;

E. 2015 Copy of RDT's Law Suit Closure showing /S/ for the U.S. Magistrate Judge's signature which RDT believes should have required full signature; Portions of Law Suit Case Document 27—nine pages; RDT's Opposition to County's Summary judgment—thirteen pages without attachments; Portions of County's Deposition consisting of ten pages with four pages of information included on four separate pages;

F. 2010 Emails from RDT's Supervisor, K.L.L. presented to Investigator S.G. - H.R. Commission and J.A. - H.R. Officer which RTD believes contradicts the 2007 Denials for promotional opportunities for RDT during EEOC's investigation by the Human Relations Commission in July 2010.

PERFORMANCE ASSESSMENT FORM

A. Probationary Midpoint (Mandatory)
B. Periodic Performance Assessment (Optional)
C. * Rating Justification (Mandatory for Above or Below Satisfactory Appraisals)

NAME: Daniels, Ruby T.
ASSESSMENT PERIOD: 09/30/03 - 09/30/04
CLASS TITLE/GRADE: Clerk Typist II/C-10
PERFORMANCE ASSESSMENT: (Supervisor must refer to appropriate duties/tasks described in employee's position description, which constitute the basis for this assessment.)

Ms. Daniels has performed her job in a manner that exceeds satisfactory during this evaluation period. She does an excellent job of data entry and makes a minimal number of mistakes. Ms. Daniels consistently enters the most calls for service each day. She frequently offers assistance with problems and complaints not directly related to the scheduling of collections. I have checked the computer records and found that Ms. Daniels has taken up to 465 calls per day with an average number of calls being 247 per day. Ms. Daniels consistently produces high quality work.

Ms. Daniels performs new tasks to improve job performance and provide for career growth with the objective of advancement. She continues with the additional responsibility by completing timesheets for the approximately 40 employees of the Collection Section. She works closely with the Crew Supervisor to ensure that all collection personnel timesheets are accurate and submitted on time.

Ms. Daniels makes suggestions and formulates new ideas contributing to the attainment of the Agency's mission, goals and objectives. She has made suggestions for the improvement of the work environment that this supervisor has implemented. Ms. Daniels willingly performs other job-related duties that are assigned by the Collection Supervisor.

SUPERVISOR'S RECOMMENDATIONS:

Ms. Daniels is encouraged to improve her computer skills by registering and completing computer training offered by the County Training Institute. Ms. Daniels needs to continue to be mindful of her tone when speaking to customers, to eliminate the perception of rudeness. She needs to maintain her professional demeanor and continue to provide a high level of customer courtesy and service.

NOTE: An employee may submit written comments to be attached to this form if received within five working days of its issuance.

Supervisor's Signature

Date

Employee's Signature

Date

* Supervisor and Employee signed original form on October 25, 2004—Information retyped for publication.

REFERENCES A. 2004
PAST PERFORMANCE APPRAISAL
Daniels, Ruby T.

Class Title	Grade	Position No.
Appraisal Period CLK TYP II	C10	04620
Department/Division	Agency/Activity	
09/30/03 – 09/30/04	#5413	

List major tasks developed from duties on position
Description Form 544
(See transmittal envelope for instructions.)% OF UN NEEDS SAT
EXC OUT   TOTAL
TIME SAT IMPR ISF EEDS STA RATING (WGT) ISFA OVE
ACT SATI NDING VALUE

Rating Point Values	0	1	2	3	4	
A DATA ENTRY/TYPING			50 X	4		= 2.00
B TELEPHONE & RECEPTION			40 X	3		= 1.20
C FILING			5 X	3		= .15
D OTHER DUTIES			5 X	3		= .15
E X						

F X
TOTAL RATING VALUE: 3.50
OVERALL APPRAISAL: EXCEEDS SATISFACTORY
ANNIVERSARY MERIT INCREASE
Anniversary Merit Increase is:
(Approved only if Overall Appraisal is Satisfactory or above)
*Approved   Not applicable   Not Approved
PROBATIONAY STATUS   Recommended permanent status
Recommended continuation of probation (Attach Justification)
Supervisor's Signature   R.W.Y. Date 10/25/04
Reviewer's Signature   M.D.   Date 11/1/04
Appointing Authority's Signature D.W. Date 01/10/05
CHECK APPROPRIATE BOXES
- ❏ I have reviewed my position description (544) and it isaccurate and current.
- ❏ I agree with this appraisal.
- ❏ I do not agree with this appraisal.
- ❏ My comments are attached.

Employee's Signature Signed RTD 10-25-04

ABOVE CHART = 0 - UNSATISFACTORY; 1 - NEEDS IM-PROVEMENT; 2 - SATISFACTORY; 3- EXCEEDS SATISFAC-TORY; 4 - OUTSTANDING - INFORMATION RETYPED FOR PUBLICATION

PERFORMANCE ASSESSMENT FORM

A. Probationary Midpoint (Mandatory)

B. Periodic Performance Assessment (Optional)

C. * Rating Justification (Mandatory for Above or Below Satisfactory Appraisals)

NAME: Thomas, Ruby D.

ASSESSMENT PERIOD: 09/30/10 - 09/30/11

CLASS TITLE/GRADE: General Clerk III/A-10

PERFORMANCE ASSESSMENT: (Supervisor must refer to appropriate duties/tasks described in employee's position description, which constitute the basis for this assessment.)

During this past performance period, Ms. Ruby Thomas has performed her duties as a General Clerk III in an "Outstanding" manner. She has demonstrated an excellent knowledge of the rules and procedures pertaining to the Collection Section as well as providing backup for her immediate Supervisor.

A. Telephone Reception: Ms. Thomas is able to provide constituents detailed information by explaining how the pickup service works and lets the constituent know what items are considered acceptable and unacceptable for pickup. She also advises the constituents where exactly to place the items in order to ensure pickup. She reminds constituents that there should not be any vehicles or anything else blocking access to the items scheduled for pickup. She answers a multi-line telephone system and handles an above average amount of calls per day. Ms. Thomas is also fully knowledgeable of the County's structure and services, which enables her to provide alternate phone numbers and agency contacts when questions arise which are out of the scope of the Collection Section.

B. Data Entry: Ms. Thomas knows the right questions to ask the constituents in order to obtain information from them so she can enter the information into the System to schedule a pickup. She is always accurate when entering information into the system. When there is a discrepancy in an address, she goes into the Tax Assessors Records and researches for correct information so that she can schedule the appointment. Once she enters the information into the system she advises the caller of the date and when and where to place the items. Ms. Thomas schedules a significant amount of the tickets in the Scheduling System. Because of her knowledge of the system, she is able to help her co-workers when they have a problem. Ms. Thomas also uses Map Quest and Yahoo in order to obtain directions to a specific address, when necessary. Ms. Thomas, as well as the other Agents, have started scheduling pickups for the Regular collection haulers.

NOTE: An employee may submit written comments to be attached to this form if received within five working days of its issuance.

PERFORMANCE ASSESSMENT: Supervisor must refer to appropriate duties/tasks described in employee's position description, which constitute the basis for this assessment.)

C. Administration: During this past appraisal period Ms. Thomas has provided clerical support to the Crew Supervisor II and Crew Supervisor III by helping them organize their filing system, creating and entering information into Excel Spreadsheets and performing other clerical duties as requested. She also produced Monthly Reports by gathering statistical information from the Driver's Inspection Reports and Worksheets. Kept track and had employees sign for gloves and other necessary supplies. She also distributed the tickets to the appropriate driver and retrieved cancelled tickets from the drivers' ticket boxes. Ms. Thomas also answered phones and took messages for the Crew Supervisors in their absence.

D. Filing/Go-Back List/E-Mails: Ms. Thomas files tickets in accordance with the established file plan. She also retrieves tickets and provides information to callers, when necessary. Ms. Thomas returns uncompleted and problem tickets to the Crew Supervisor and follows up to ensure the issue is resolved. She files the tickets in the correct manner under the appropriate date for easy retrieval. Ms. Thomas prepares the Go-back list daily in a timely manner and provides each Agent with a copy as well as giving the actual tickets and a copy of the list to the Crew Supervisor III. Ms. Thomas also schedules appointments through the email system.

E. Training: Ms. Thomas attends all mandatory training and actively participants sharing her thoughts and Opinions.

F. Performs Other Duties: Ms. Thomas is willing to help out whenever necessary. Ms. Thomas prints out the daily tickets for distribution to the Collection Section, there is a staff shortage. She also provides backup for her supervisor performing various duties, as necessary, allowing for the continued efficient operation of the section. She is capable of multitasking and demonstrates her capabilities on a daily basis. Ms. Thomas is an asset to the Division and the Department and it is reflected by her knowledge of overall County functions and that of the Collection Management Group in order to provide valuable information regarding the Collection Section as well as information on other agencies in the County Government to the citizens of the County.

Supervisor's Signature

Date

Employee's Signature

Date

(RDT) REFERENCES A. 2011 PLANTATION MENTALITY PAST PERFORMANCE APPRAISAL   Name   Emp. ID No. COUNTY, MD THOMAS, RUBY D. 1111011297

Appraisal Period

09/30/10 - 09/30/11 List major tasks developed from duties on position Description Form 544

(See transmittal envelope for instructions.)

Rating Point Values   0   1   2   3   4

A TELEPHONE RECEPTION

B DATA ENTRY

C ADMINISTRATION

D FILING/GO BACK LISTIE-MAILING

E TRAINING

F PERFORMS OTHER DUTIES

30 X   X

20 X 15X 25 X 5X

5X

TOTAL RATING VALUE:

3.0

OVERALL APPRAISAL: OUTSTANDING

ANNIVERSARY MERIT INCREASE

Anniversary Merit Increase is:

(Approved only if Overall Appraisal is Satisfactory or above)

Approved   *Not applicable

Not Approved

PROBATIONARY STATUS

Recommended permanent status

Recommended continuation of probation Attach Justification

CHECK APPROPRIATE BOXES

Supervisor's Signature   K.L.

Date 09/14/11

* I have reviewed my position description (544) and it is accurate and current.

Reviewer's Signature   A.A.W Date

* I agree with this appraisal.

I do not agree with this appraisal

Appointing Authority's Signature

Date

My comments are attached.

Employee's Signature

Signed Ruby D. Thomas 09/14/11

PLEASE NOTE:

(THIS APPRAISAL WAS CHANGED BY D.B. ACTING DIRECTOR, FROM AN OUTSTANDING RATING WHICH HAD BEEN SUBMITTED FOR RDT BY K.L. SUPERVISOR, TO SATISFACTORY BUT THE SUPERVISOR, K.L. WOULD ONLY CHANGE THE RATING TO EXCEED SATISFACTORY IN SEPTEMBER 2011) SEE COPY OF RESUBMISSION OF APPRAISAL DTD. NOV. 2011 SIGNED BY D.B. ACTING DIRECTOR.

ABOVE CHART = 0 - UNSATISFACTORY; 1- NEEDS IMPROVEMENT; 2 - SATISFACTORY; 3 - EXCEEDS SATISFACTORY; 4 - OUTSTANDING - INFORMATION RETYPED FOR PUBLICATION

REFERENCES B. 2004-2005 -
CLERICAL STAFF CLASSIFICATIONS

AGENCY RESTRUCTURE PLAN PHASE TWO
List of Employees Whose Position will be Reallocated

Incumbent		Division Current /Section Classification	Proposed Classification	Position Number
13.	L.C.	W. Mgt. General Clerk II	General Clerk III	02836*
14.	R.T.D.	W. Mgt. Clerk Typist	General Clerk III	04620
15.	D.F.	W. Mgt. General Clerk II	General Clerk III	07301
16.	J.M.	W. Mgt. Public Service Aide II	General Clerk III	04937

**LIST OF EMPLOYEE'S POSITIONS REALLOCATED BETWEEN 2004 -2005

1.	Admin. Svs.	Engineering Tech III	Engineering Tech IV	06300
2.	E. Svs.	Engineer III	Engineer IV	06899
3.	E. Svs.	Admin. Asst. III	Admin. Asst.	02463
4.	E. Svs.	Planner III	Planner IV	06347
5.	E. Svs.	Planner V	Engineer V	06360
6.	E. Svs.	Planner III	Planner IV	06158
7.	E. Sys.	Engineer IV	Engineer V	07040
8.	E. Svs.	Admin. Aide HI	Admin. Aide IV	00494
9.	P.&R.	Engineer IV	Engineer V	06359
10.	P.&R.	Admin. Spec. II	Associate Director	06343
11.	P.&R.	Engineer III	Engineer V	06299
12.	P.&R.	Engineer III	Engineer IV	06297

* Position remained General Clerk II - L.C. retired before effective promotion date

REFERENCES C. 1997 – 2005
COUNTY PERSONNEL INFORMATION DOCUMENT
NAME: DANIELS, RUBY T.

Action/ Step	Grade/ Number	Position/ Pay	Hourly/ Salary	Annual/ Title	Class/ Date	Hire/	Type
1.New Hire	G15/A	09420	11.49	23,903	Paralegal Asst.		09/29/97
Employment Status: LTerm no benefits							
2.Prob-F/T	C-8	04620	9.78	18,736	Clk. Typist		03/30/98
Employment Status: Active Full Time							
3.Cost of Living	C-8	04620	9.25	19,251	Clk. Typist		07/05/98
Employment Status: Active Full Time							
4.Chg. To PERM-F/T		04620	10.20	21,225	Clk. Typist		09/30/98
Employment Status: Active Full Time							
5.Cost of Living		04620	14.77	30,719	Clk. Typist		04/03/05
Employment Status: Active Full Time							
6.Promotion*		04620	14.77	30,719	Gen. Clk. III		07/10/05
Employment Status: Active Full Time *Back dated document indicating promotion with no increase							
7.Merit Increase		04620	15.29	31,794	Clk. Typist*		09/30/05
Employment Status: Active Full Time *Title was changed to Gen. Clk III on 11/27/05; promotion date was backdated to 07/10/05 with no monetary increase.							
8.Promotion		04620	15.29	31,794	Gen. Clk III		11/27/05
Employment Status: Active Full Time; Salary changed due to Merit Increase 9/30/05 not a promotional increase as document indicates a salary change.							

REFERENCES D. CYBORG PRINT OUT INDICATING TRANSFER OF RDT INTO GENERAL CLERK POSITION

NAME: RUBY D. THOMAS
SALARY ASSIGNMENT/CHANGES
PRIOR SALARY CHANGES
INC

NBR	Date	Type of Change	Frequency Rates	Hours	Salary
*01	11-27-05	S08 Transfer	Bi Weekly 15.2858	80.00	1,222.86
01	09-30-06	I15 Merit Increase	Bi Weekly 15.8208	80.00	1,265.66
01	09-30-05	I15 Merit Increase	Bi Weekly 15.2858	80.00	1,222.86
*01	07-10-05	S08 Transfer	Bi Weekly 14.7689	80.00	1,181.51
01	04-03-05	I55 Cost of Living	COBi Weekly14.7689	80.00	1,181.51
01	01-09-05	I55 Cost of Living	CO Bi Weekly14.6227	80.00	1,169.82
01	10-03-04	I55 Cost of Living	CO Bi Weekly14.4779	80.00	1,158.23
01	09-30-04	I15 Merit Increase	Bi Weekly 14.3346	80.00	1,146.77
01	04-04-04	I55 Cost of Living	CO Bi Weekly13.8499	80.00	1,107.99
01	01-11-04	I55 Cost of Living	CO Bi Weekly13.7128	80.00	1,097.02

07-01-05	Change Union to 2462 – Same Money		
07-10-05	COLA 14.7689 to 15.1381		
09-30-05	MERIT	15.6679	
07-09-06	COLA	16.0596	
09-30-06	MERIT	16.6217	

REFERENCES E.
2015 PORTIONS OF LAW SUIT CLOSURE AND COURT ORDER FROM A U.S. MAGISTRATE JUDGE IN THE UNITED STATES DISTRICT COURT FOR THE DISTRICT OF MARYLAND

RUBY DEE THOMAS

v.

Civil No. 13-326

COUNTY, MARYLAND *

ORDER

In accordance with the foregoing Memorandum. and for the reasons set forth therein, it is, this 23rd day of January. 2015, by the United States District Court for the District of Maryland, ORDERED:

1. That Defendant's Motion for Summary Judgment, ECF No. 17, BE and the same hereby IS, GRANTED.
2. The Clerk is directed to close this case.

United States Magistrate Judge

2015 PORTIONS OF LAW SUIT CLOSURE AND COURT ORDER FROM A U.S. MAGISTRATE JUDGE

Case 8:13-cv-00326-   Document 27 Filed 01/23115 Page 1 of 9
IN THE UNITED STATES DISTRICT COURT
FOR THE DISTRICT OF MARYLAND
RUBY DEE THOMAS
Civil No.   13-326
COUNTY, MARYLAND *
MEMORANDUM OPINION

Presently pending is Defendant's Motion for Summary Judgment. ECF No. 17. The issues have been fully briefed and no hearing is necessary. See Local Rule 105.6. For the reasons set forth below, Defendant's motion will be granted.

1. Procedural History.

On January 30, 2013, Plaintiff filed a one count complaint alleging that Defendant retaliated against her for engaging in the protected activity of filing a discrimination charge with the County Human Relations Commission (the Commission). ECF No. 1. After Plaintiff was deemed to be proceeding pro se, ECF No. 11., the parties jointly consented to proceed before a United States Magistrate Judge. ECF Nos. 13 and 16. Defendant then filed the pending motion.

1. Background.

The following facts are either undisputed or are construed in the light most favorable to Plaintiff. In 1998, Plaintiff, Ruby Dee Thomas,' began her employment with Defendant, County as a "Clerk Typist 1/II." ECF No. 17-1 at 4; No. 19 at 1. Plaintiff worked in the Collection division within the County's Department of __ In 2005, the Department restructured several positions within the division as part of an agency-wide reorganization. According to an audit conducted prior to the reorganization, Plaintiff's duties were consistent with the duties of a General Clerk III and thus, during the reorganization, Plaintiff's position was reclassified from a Clerk Typist I/ II to a General Clerk III. ECF No. 17-2 at 3; No. 20 at 4. "Plaintiff was the Senior Employee during the reallocation and 10% salary increases were given to the two Caucasian employees, not the one Black employee - the Plaintiff." ECF No. 19 at 2. Defendant does not dispute that employees who were previously classified as a General Clerk II received a 10% increase in pay when they were reclassified to General Clerk III. This occurred, according to Defendant, because, during the audit, it was determined that employees who were classified as General Clerk II were also performing the duties of the General Clerk III, and Plaintiff did not receive a pay increase because the Clerk Typist II position she occupied was already in a comparable grade with the General Clerk III position. ECF No. 17-2 at 3. The parties agree that Plaintiff was the highest paid General Clerk III within the Collection Section at that time of the agency reorganization, even without an increase in pay. Id; ECF No. 20 at 7.

In December 2006, Plaintiff filed a discrimination charge against Defendant with the Commission alleging race and age discrimination as well as retaliation. ECF No. 1 at 2. The charge was dismissed as untimely by the Equal Employment Opportunity Commission (EEOC) on February 1, 2007. ECF No. -1 at 2.

In February 2007, July 2007, November 2007, and April 2010, Plaintiff's supervisor submitted Plaintiffs name for promotion to the General Clerk IV position, but Plaintiff was not promoted. ECF No. 20 at 9; ECF No. 20-14 at 5; ECF No. 17-2 at 3. On June 15, 2010. Plaintiff filed a new EEOC charge claiming that Defendant retaliated against her in denying the April 2010 promotion. ECF No. 20 at 9. The Commission was "unable to conclude that the information obtained establishes violations of the statutes." Footnote 2) ECF No. 1 at 3.

2.   Standard of Review.

Pursuant to Rule 56(c) of the Federal Rules of Civil Procedure, summary judgment is appropriate "if the pleadings, depositions, answers to interrogatories, and admissions on file, together with the affidavits, if any, show that there is no genuine issue as to any material fact and that the moving party is entitled to judgment as a matter of law.".An-derson v. Liberty Lobby, Inc.. 477 U.S. 343, 347 (1986), "For pur-poses of summary judgment, a fact is material if, when applied to the substantive law, it affects the outcome of the litigation." Nero v. Bal-timore Cnty. MD. 512 F. Supp. 2d 407, 409 (D.Md.2007)(citing An-derson, 477 U.S. at 248). "Summary judgment is also appropriate when a party 'fails to make a showing sufficient to establish the exis-tence of an element essential to that party's case, and on which that party will bear the burden of proof at trial.'" Laura Campbell Trust v. John Hancock- Life Ins. Co_. 411 F. Supp. 2d 606, 609 (D. Md. 2006) (quoting Celotex Corp v. Catrell, 477 U.S. 317, 322 (1986).

A party opposing a properly supported motion for summary judg-ment bears the burden of establishing the existence of a genuine issue of material fact. Anderson. 477 U.S. at 248-49. "When a motion for summary judgment is made and supported as provided in [Rule 56], an adverse party may not rest upon the mere allegations or denials of the adverse party's pleading, but the adverse party's response, by af-fidavit or as otherwise provided in [Rule 56] must set forth specific facts showing that there is a genuine issue for trial." Bertrand v. Chil-dren's Home. 489 F.Supp.2d 516, 518 (D. Md. 2007) (citing Fed. R. Civ. P. 56(e)). "The facts, as well as the justifiable inferences to be drawn therefrom, must be viewed in the light most favorable to the nonmoving party." Id. at 518-19 (citing Matsushita Elec. Indus. Co. v. Zenith Radio Corp., 475

U.S. 574. 587-88 (1986). "The court, however, cannot rely upon unsupported speculation and it has an affirmative obligation to pre-vent factually unsupported claims and defenses from proceeding to trial." Id. at 519 (citing Felty v. Graves-Humphreys Co_ 818 F.2d 1126, 1128 (4th Cir. (1987)).

Plaintiff is currently proceeding as a pro se litigant. "Although pro se litigants are to be given some latitude, the above standards apply to everyone." Smith v. Vilsack, 832 F. Supp.2d 573. 580 (D.Md. 2011). "Thus, as courts have recognized repeatedly, even a pro se party may not avoid summary judgment by relying on bald assertions and speculative arguments." Id. (citations omitted).

3. Discussion.

Defendant argues that summary judgment is warranted because (1) Plaintiff's June 2010 retaliation claim is untimely with regard to the February 2007, July 2007, and November 2007 requests for promotion; (2) there is no temporal proximity, and thus no causal connection, between Plaintiffs 2006 charge of discrimination and the April 2010 denial of a promotion; and (3) in any event, the County's budgetary constraint qualifies as a legitimate, non-discriminatory reason for the promotion being denied. ECF No. 17 at 5-7. Plaintiff responds that her discrimination claim was timely because she was not aware of the three 2007 promotion requests until 2010 and Defendant's justification of budgetary constraint is invalid because the constraint only applied to certain employees. ECF No. 20 at 9, 11.

A Title VII plaintiff "may defeat a defendant's motion for summary judgment and establish a claim for intentional race, sex, or age discrimination or retaliation through either the 'mixed-motive' or 'pretext' methods of proof." Kess v. Mun. Employees Credit Union of Baltimore, Inc., 319 F. Supp. 2d 637, 643 (D. Md. 2004). "Under the mixed-motive method, a plaintiff avoids summary judgment by introducing sufficient direct or circumstantial evidence for a reasonable jury to conclude that an impermissible factor actually motivated an adverse employment decision." Id. Plaintiff has not presented any direct or circumstantial evidence showing that race actually motivated an adverse employment decision. Accordingly, Plaintiffs claim will be analyzed using the "pretext" methodology.

Under the traditional "pretext * method of proof, a plaintiff establishes her claim using a burden-shifting framework. McDonnell Douglas Corp. v. Green, 411 U.S. 792. 802-05 (1973). To survive summary judgment under this scheme, Plaintiff must demonstrate (1) that she engaged in protected conduct, (2) that she suffered an adverse action, and (3) that a causal link exists between the protected conduct and the adverse action. Smith v. Vilsack, 832 F.Supp. 2d 573, 585 (D.Md.2011 (citations omitted). Once that challenge is met, the burden shifts to Defendant to provide a non-discriminatory explanation for the adverse action. Id. If Defendant does so, then he burden shifts back to Plaintiff to show that the proffered reason is pretextual. Id.

A. Timeliness of Plaintiff's Retaliation Claim.

Plaintiff's claim is untimely as to the promotion denials occurring in 2007. The protected activity cited by Plaintiff is the lodging of a discrimination complaint in December 2006. ECF No. 17-4. Title VII, the basis of Plaintiffs claim, requires a charge to be filed within 300 days of the alleged discriminatory act. 42 U.S.C. § 2000e-5(e). Plaintiff did not file her charge until June 15. 2010, far more than 300 days after the 2007 actions. Plaintiff's claim is thus untimely as to those actions. Soble v. Univ of Maryland, 572 F. Supp, 1509, 1512 (D. Md. 1983).

Plaintiff asserts that her claim should be considered timely because she was not timely aware of the 2007 promotion requests. ECF No. 20 at 9. However, in her deposition Plaintiff testified that she "knew every time that [Ms. L.] submitted" a recommendation for her promotion. ECF No. 26-1 at 4. She reiterated that in 2007 I did know because [Ms. L said she was submitting it." Id.at5. Plaintiff cannot excuse the delinquency of her filing based on a lack of notice.

Plaintiff also contends that Defendant's conduct was continuous in nature and thus the time period in which she may file her retaliation claim should be tolled. ECF No. 1at 3; ECF No. 20 at 11. Title VII recognizes that certain violations, once commenced, are continuing in nature, and in such a scenario, plaintiffs can file charges at any time up to 300 days after the violation ceases. United Air Lines, Inc. v. Evans, 431 U.S. 553, 561 (1977). However, this is not such a case. In Soble v. Univ. of Maryland, 572 F.Supp. 1509 (D.Md. 1983), the court held that "plaintiff's claim of discrimination in denial of promotion arose each time she was denied the promotion, and, because of this, the [earlier] decision not to recommend the plaintiff for promotion [wa]s barred as the subject of a Title VII claim." Id.at 1516. The court emphasized that "[w]hile the plaintiff has continued her efforts to obtain a promotion, continuing efforts does not mean that a continuing violation is present." Id. The court accordingly dismissed the claim arising from the earlier denial of promotion. The same result is warranted here with regard to the 2007 promotion requests. The claim is timely only as to the 2010 promotion request.

B. A Prima Facie Retaliation Claim: Establishing a Causal Link.

Having eliminated the 2007 promotion denials from consideration, the court will consider whether a causal link exists between the 2006 charge of discrimination and the denial of the April 2010 request for a promotion. Ordinarily there must be "some degree of temporal proximity to suggest a causal connection." Constantine v. Rectors & Visitors of George Mason Univ., 411 F.3d 474,501 (4th Cir. 2005). A lengthy time lapse between the protected activity and the alleged adverse action often negates any inference that a causal connection exists between the two. Murphy-Taylor v. Hofmann, 968 F.Supp.2d 693, 720 (D.Md.2013). "Although the Fourth Circuit has not set a clear limit for 'close temporal proximity,' it has required other evidence of discriminatory animus when the interval between protected activity and the adverse action is as great as seven months." Lee v. Safeway, Inc.. No.RDB 13-3476, 2014 WL 4926183, at *12 D.Md. Sept.30,2014)(citing Lettieri v. Equant Inc. 478 F.3d 640, 650 (4th Cir. 2007); see also Pascual v. Lowe's Home Centers, Inc.. 193 Fed. App'x. 229, 233 (4th Cir. 2006) (concluding that a lapse of three to four months between the protected activity and the alleged retaliation "is too long to establish a causal connection by temporal proximity alone"). Here, the 2010 promotion denial occurred more than three years after Plaintiff filed her 2006 charge of discrimination. This time gap is too long to establish a causal connection between Plaintiffs discrimination charge and Defendant's refusal to promote. See Hawkins-v. Leggett, 955 F. Supp. 2d 474.488 (D. Md. 2013) ("Temporal proximity of six months, however, is insufficient to state a prima facie case of causation.").

Plaintiff also points to the facts that (1) she had been employed by Defendant for seven years when her Department was restructured, (2) she was the most senior employee of all of the clerks, and (3) she was the only clerk responsible for performing supervisory duties such as documenting time sheets, producing weekly reports and training new staff, as evidence that she should have received an increase in pay. Her supervisor, K.L. confirmed that she requested a promotion for Plaintiff "because when I am out of the office [Plaintiff] acts as the Lead Clerk." ECF No. 20-22 at 3. This evidence, like much of Plaintiff's evidence, may have been relevant to a discrimination claim, but it is not relevant to this retaliation claim. (Footnote 3 was indicated)

C. Evidence of a Legitimate Non-Discriminatory Justification.
Even if Plaintiff had successfully raised a presumption of retaliation. Defendant has satisfied its burden of providing a legitimate non-discriminatory reason for denying Plaintiffs requests for promotion, namely, that the Department was restricted by a budgetary constraint. See Eduardo Vasquez v. Maryland Port Admin. 937 F. Supp. 517 522 (D. Md. 1995) (concluding that budgetary considerations, staffing and other operational requirements constituted legitimate, non-discriminatory reasons for denying a request for training and were necessary for effective business administration). J.A., the human resources officer for the Department, stated in an affidavit that Plaintiff was not promoted to the General Clerk IV position in February 2007, July 2007, November 2007 or April 2010 "due to budget constraints imposed by the County's Office of Management and Budget." ECF No. 17-2 at 3. Ms. A affirmed that "other County employees within [the Department] were also submitted for promotion in February 2007, July 2007, November 2007 and April 2010" and "[l]ike Mrs. Thomas, none of those employees were [sic] promoted due to budget constraints imposed by the County's Office of Management and Budget." ECF No. 26-2 at 2. "In fact, all requests from employees involving fiscal salary adjustments, promotions, etc were held in abeyance due to the fiscal constraints imposed by the County's Office of Management and Budget." Id.at 3. Plaintiff has offered no evidence to rebut Ms. A assertions or otherwise show that the claimed budgetary constraint is actually a pretext for retaliation. (Footnote 4) The fact, if correct, that Plaintiff was asked to train two Caucasian employees in 2006. ECF No. 20 at 5-6, is not relevant because it is remote in time

and because these employees are not shown to have occupied comparable positions. Thus, Defendant's justification for denying Plaintiffs 2010 promotion request remains unopposed.

4. Conclusion.
The Court will grant Defendant's motion for summary judgment.

Date: January 23, 2015   United States Magistrate Judge

REFERENCES E.
OPPOSITION TO COUNTY'S SUMMARY JUDGMENT
IN THE UNITED STATES DISTRICT COURT
FOR THE DISTRICT OF MARYLAND

RUBY DEE THOMAS
Plaintiff,

Vs.   CASE NO. 13-CV-326

COUNTY, MARYLAND
Defendant.

Page 1 of 13

Plaintiffs Memorandum In Opposition of Defendant's Motion for Summary Judgment

Plaintiff opposes Defendant's Memorandum requesting summary judgment on all claims against it, dated November 17, 2014.

FACTS

Plaintiff filed the last charge of discrimination for retaliation against the Defendant on June 15, 2010 signed by Plaintiff through the Human Relations Commission. An ADR (Alternative Disposition Resolution) form was also signed by the

Plaintiff and Intake/Investigator J M. V; There were four letters acknowledging assignments of Plaintiff's complaint from the Human Relations Commission.

(Attachment 1- Letters from Investigators S.G. - 10/15/10 & 07/14/11; JM. V- .02/28/11; and H.H. 12/02/10) (Attachment 2 - Intake Interview Form indicating Plaintiff's signature regarding ADR.)

Plaintiff was a covered employee under Title VII under Enforcement and Penalties [29 CFR-1620.27] which indicates a lawsuit under State or Federal district Court can be filed. Plaintiff's rights under Labor Organizations [29 U.S.C.206(d)(2),(4)] were disregarded when Plaintiff's title was changed in November 2005 with a document indicating promotion and backdated to July 2005 indicating the same with no monetary increase.

Plaintiff was hired on March 30, 1998, as a Clerk Typist I/II. At the time of hiring date with the Department of __the Plaintiffs name was Ruby T. Daniels. Today, Plaintiff uses her maiden name Ruby Dee Thomas. The married name is Ruby Dee Thomas-Blackmon. Plaintiff's first 6 months of employment was for a probationary period as a Clerk Typist I until September 30, 1998. As outlined in the Letter of Employment dated March, 17, 1998, Plaintiff was non-competitively promoted to Clerk Typist II position No. was 04620. (Letter of Plaintiff's qualifications as an Administrative Aide dated March 29, 1997. Also, a letter qualifying Plaintiff as the Clerk Typist I/II and dated March 29, 1997). (Attachment 3- Qualification Letters). ARGUMENT

Defendant failed to abide by the Agreement between __County, Maryland and Council 67, American Federation of State, County and Municipal Employees, AFL-CIO and Ifs Affiliated Locals 1170, (2462), 2735, and 3389. Plaintiff was a member of Local 2462.

Plaintiff had been employed by the same Department of __ for 7 (seven) years when the decision to restructure the Collection Section Call Center, claiming all 4 Clerks performed the same duties and the Administrative personnel decided to change the position descriptions of all 4 Clerks.

The four Clerks held titles as follows: one Clerk Typist II- Plaintiff was Black; two General Clerk 11- one Caucasian and one Black; and one Public Service Aide II-Caucasian. The organization chart shows a revised date of 5/23/05 outlining 4 GC (General Clerk - III) under Customer Service.

(Attachment 4- __ County Organizational Chart) The effective promotion date for all staff, at the time of restructuring was November 27, 2005 but, the Chart indicates a revised date of May 23, 2005 indicating incorrect information. Upon Plaintiff's receipt of the first Position Information Document (PID), it indicated promotion effective date was November 27, 2005. Plaintiff can prove there was no monetary increase although documentation indicated Promotion. (Attachment 5 Plaintiff's first PID) Plaintiff filed a grievance requesting a 10% increase. (Attachment 6 - Grievance dated January 5, 2006)

The employee in position No. 02836 never received the change to GC-III because that individual retired in May 2005 before November 27, 2005 and that position remained a GC-I/II. (Attachment 4 - Organizational Chart) Upon retirement of that Position No. 02836 , Plaintiff became the Senior employee. (Attachment 7 - Article 23 - Seniority County/Union Agreement)

Union Representatives, J.D and P. F were the Union Representatives responsible for submission of Plaintiff's filed Grievance. The Grievance only went through Steps 1-2 and a Grievance has 4 steps before arbitration. (Attachment 8 - Article 46 -- Grievance Procedure) After filing the Grievance in January 2006, Plaintiff received the second Position Information Document (PID) in May 2006 backdating the November 27, 2005 date of promotion to July 10, 2005. Why were the promotions backdated? The Plaintiff waited 4 months before finally signing the position description which could have been considered as a delay for promotion of other staff or a retaliatory action against the Plaintiff for waiting that long to sign. The two employees who were promoted received four months of back pay but, the Plaintiff only receive the Second PID indicating promotion with no monetary increase. (Attachment 9 - Plaintiffs Second PID),

Plaintiff never received a PID indicating she had been Transfered into the position of GC-III but, documentation of such action was amongst copies received upon request of personnel file (Attachment 10 - Information showing two dates for Plaintiff being Transferred into the Position of GC- III not a Promotion utilizing the same dates November 27, 2005 and July 10, 2005) Plaintiff was never advised of the changes.

During the restructuring of the Collection Section in 2005, Plaintiff received email requests from J.A., Human Resource Officer (HRO)- between December 2004 through May 2005, but did not sign the position description as requested. (Attachment 11 - All email requests from HRO - J.A.) The HRO was also responsible for responding to the EEOC's request for information at a hearing with S G Investigator, Human Relations Commission on July 14, 2010. (Attachment 12 –S.G.) regarding Plaintiffs retaliation charge. The

70

HRO should not have been requested to provide this information because Plaintiff rejected all requests for signature to move forward during the restructuring.of the Collections Section and it was a problem and that is when Retaliation began against the Plaintiff for continual rejection of the signing of the position description at the request of J..A, HRO. (Attachment - 13 Request for Information from EEOC)

The Supervisory Clerk position became vacant after September 2002 through 2004 and assignments of duties that were performed by the Supervisory Clerk were transferred to the Clerk Typist by R.Y. Collection Supervisor, Management Division. Plaintiff's evaluations are documented from 2002 through 2004 assigning certain responsibilities to the Plaintiff and no other staff were responsible for the different assignments but the Plaintiff, i.e. documenting time sheets for approximately 40 or more staff in Collection Section; production of daily tickets, weekly reports, training new staff personnel and any other administrative duties that were the responsibility of the Supervisory Clerk. (Attachment 14 - Evaluations 2002 through 2004)

In the year 2006, CS (Caucasian) was assigned to the Collection Section, and previously held the title of Executive Administrative Aide, stayed in the Collection Section less than one year salary ranged over $75,000 per year. The Aide advised Plaintiff that she never supervised anyone but, Plaintiff was assigned the responsibility of training this individual. (Attachment 4-Organizational Chart)

September 2006, KL, (Caucasian) Plaintiff's Supervisor was assigned to the Collection Section, her salary ranged the same as the Executive Administrative Aide, $72,000 or more and, the Plaintiff was asked to train this Supervisor by the Acting Associate Director, R.H. Mr. H signed the Plaintiff's Grievance in January 2006 and convinced the Plaintiff to finally sign the Position Description that the HRO had presented to him to get Plaintiff's signature during the restructuring of the Collection Section. As previously mentioned, the Plaintiff was not aware of Supervisor's submission of request to promote in February, July and November 2007 until receipt of documents from Plaintiff's request for Personnel File and after the defendant's failure to promote again in April 2010. Plaintiff filed the last Discrimination Charge in June 2010, claiming retaliation.

Plaintiff was a union member under AFSCME Local (2462) and was not privileged with the right to bargain collectively subject to the terms and conditions of the negotiated labor Agreement.

The binding union agreement during the reallocation was not carried out by County personnel responsible for making the position changes. The Defendant's Acting Director wrote a response to the EEOC in a letter dated January 24, 2007, "Ms. Daniels filed an official grievance against the Department requesting that the Department "make her whole" by granting a 10% increase in her base salary. Please note: Employee #04937 had only worked permanently 1 year 6 months with a position titled Public Service Aide in the Collection Section but,managed to be promoted from a C-4 to a C-10 (Caucasian) GC III. Employee #07301 (Caucasian) was a GC-II and had worked 4 years 6 months in. Yes, the Plaintiff was the highest paid General Clerk in the Collection Section because she had worked 7 years 10 months in the same office when the reallocations were initiated. (Attachment 15 - Information Outlining 3 in (Attachment 15-a Letter from the Acting Director dated January 24, '07 Response to EEOC in Baltimore

Plaintiff Did Timely Exhaust Her Administrative Remedies

Plaintiff provided Defendant with all necessary documents regarding the promotion issues but, Plaintiff's facts were not taken into consideration and the County Government officials disregarded discrimination laws.

The Human Resource Officer of which an affidavit is included in the Defendant's Motion for Summary Judgment, was one of management's team personnel that Plaintiff rejected emails of request for signing the position description.

In a letter of response to Philadelphia's EEOC office dated March 8, 2012, Plaintiff responded to a Disposition/Substantial Weight Review Notice FEPA Charge No: IV10-0610 regarding the Retaliation Case filed in June 2010. Plaintiff responded to the Notice dated March 5, 2012 and asked that this case be investigated by an outsider since the Human Relations Commission was located in a County building and Plaintiff feared it could be a conflict of interest. (Attachment 16 - Plaintiffs Response to Charge No. ..117-10-0610).

The EEOC Investigative team referred all requests for information regarding Plaintiff's case to J.A.,HRO to provide the Human Relations Commission with documented proof of non- retaliatory actions which was needed to try to prove that the Plaintiff had no documented proof of retaliation. If all information was taken into consideration and properly reviewed by an outsider as Plaintiff requested in the Weight Review Notice this case would have a different resolution. Note: J.A., HRO was the individual the Plaintiff continuously refused certain information requests.

It took the Human Relations Commission 21 months to respond to the Plaintiff's case. An ADR (Alternative Disposition Resolution) was signed by Plaintiff on June 15, 2010.

Plaintiff filed a lawsuit after receipt of a letter from -U.S. Equal Employment Opportunity Commission's Dismissal and Notice of Rights from the Philadelphia District Office located at 801 Market St. Suite 1300 and signed by S.H. dated November 2, 2012. (Attachment 17 - Letter Of Dismissal & Right to Sue)

Union Representatives failed to carry out the Plaintiffs grievance in a timely manner from January 2006 through November 2006, Plaintiff contacted the EEOC in Baltimore, Md. in November 2006, and Plaintiff received documents indicating failure to respond within 300 days. (Attachment 18 - Cases Interpreting Title VII - Edelman v. Lynchburg College, 122 S. Ct. 1145 (2002). Plaintiff received a questionnaire in November 2006 and received documents in December 2006 to determine whether a case could be filed. Plaintiff believes the case should have been acknowledged in November 2006 when the questionnaire was sent from EEOC. If the Form, to file a case was sent in November along with the questionnaire, Plaintiff should have been privileged with filing before the 300 day requirement.

Defense team needed to review documents regarding how long the last case filed through the Human Relations Commission took before indicating Plaintiff failed to file a charge of discrimination within 180 days of the alleged misconduct. The February, July, and November 2007 promotion request were initiated by Plaintiff's Supervisor, K.L. Plaintiff became aware of the three 2007 promotion requests after the investigation with the Human Relations Commission's hearing and Plaintiff's Supervisor did submit this information during the hearing conducted by SG, Investigator for Human Relations Commission. The Plaintiff, at this time filed the Retaliation charge with Human Relations Commission so the dates of harm referred to by the Defense were not dates of harm that the Plaintiff was aware of. Plaintiff filed with the Human Relations Commission for Retaliation on June 15, 2010 because of the failure to promote in April 2010. Plaintiff filed 52 days after denial of the last request for promotion as outlined in the information provided to JA, HRO from K. L. (Attachment 19 - Email dated July 7, 2010) This request for Information was from EEOC sent to IA-, HRO for information regarding the Plaintiff. (Attachment 20 - EEOC's Information Request on Plaintiff)

Plaintiff performed duties of an Administrative Aide from June 28, 2010 through July 2011 and Management staff was sent an email outlining the request from VC.L. (Attachment 21-Email Dated June 25, 2010 - Assignment). with no monetary increase being initiated as outlined in the County/Union Agreement. (Attachment 22 - Article 18 - Temporary Assignments) When an employee is required to perform all or any part of the duties of a higher job classification after one (1) work day they shall be compensated retroactively at the rate of ten percent (10%) above their current salary or the minimum necessary to place the employee at the entry level of that grade or whichever is greater. No employee shall be required to perform such work for more than one hundred twenty (120) calendar days in any one (1) calendar year. The employee shall receive a performance assessment if they remain in the higher classification for more than thirty (30) days. (Attachment 23 - Evaluation)

Plaintiff was reassigned to the General Clerk III position after a meeting in the last week of July 2011 with her immediate Supervisor, KL and the Crew Supervisor. Plaintiff declined the request to perform both duties since no monetary increase had taken effect as outlined in the County/Union Agreement.

A memorandum dated July 16, 2012, was advertised requesting volunteers, if interested, to work in the 311 Call Center, Plaintiff and one other Collection employee did not volunteer. Two other staff members volunteered. A meeting was held by the Outgoing Director, S.W and an Assistant Associate Director, BW and letters were presented to all four.Collection General Clerk III to report to the Office of Community Relations on October 1, 2012. Since the Administrative Aide position was vacant, Plaintiff requested to remain at the Landfill and fill the position of Administrative Aide but, the request was denied and a Union Representative, S.B was present at this meeting. The Call Center Representative General Clerk IV position was a non-union G-12 position but required English and Spanish to qualify and be able to read and write in both languages. (Attachment 24 - Call Center Job Announcement) This was supposedly a volunteer position but, all staff in the Collections Call Center were transferred regardless.

CONCLUSION

A continuing violation, as outlined in the 2010 Charge of Discrimination for Retaliation should be established showing __. County, Maryland, Defendant engaged in an express policy of unlawful discrimination and continuously failed to abide by the Union/County Agreement resulting in reckless indifference to the Federally protected rights of an aggrieved individual union member and that the Defendant also engaged in unlawful intentional wrongdoing, maliciously and fraudulently damaging chances of future upward mobility and a disregard for employment advancement, demonstrating discrimination of the Civil Rights Act of 1991 and Section 101 Title I of the Federal Civil Rights Remedies Section 1977 of revised Statues (42 USC 1981(a). (__The Agency)_ experienced budget constraints imposed by the County's Office of Management and Budget only for certain employees. Eighteen employees had left the Agency within Collections when Plaintiffs position was continuously being submitted for consideration and should have been applied as the Agreement outlined, yet none of management staff responsible for carrying out Plaintiff's possibility for upward mobility were concerned. The Supervisory Clerk-Black left in the year 2002 salary ranged approximately $39,000. It seemed to be a problem with the salary range for certain personnel. Plaintiff's salary at retirement in 2012 was approximately $38,000. Review salaries paid to the two Caucasian Administrative Aide salaries ranging $75,000 and were trained by a General Clerk III - the Plaintiff yet, no consideration for a 10% increase after working 14 years 6 months. Something is wrong with this County

Government Agency and no one is taking action to resolve the issue. As a matter of law, the Defendant should not be entitled to Summary Dismissal and Plaintiff has put forth direct evidence of retaliation and opposes Motion for Summary Judgment. Therefore, the Plaintiff should be entitled to judgment and ask that the Court be the deciding factor regarding Opposition by the Counsel for the Defendant.

Respectfully submitted,

_____
RUBY DEE THOMAS, Plaintiff Pro Se

Sent: Wednesday, July 07, 2010 12:21 PM
To: K.L.L. - Administrative Asst.
Subject: EEOC Complaint
Importance: High
Hello A. - RC Supervisor

Please call me at your earliest convenience. I am responding to request for information from the Human Relations Commission concerning a complaint received from that office filed by Ruby Thomas.

Thanks!
J. - HR Officer

From: K.L.L. - Administrative Asst.
Sent: Wednesday, July 07, 2010 1:32 PM
To: J.R.A. - HR Officer
Subject: RE: EEOC Complaint
Here are some Bullets on Ruby Thomas:
- o Sent e-mail to Mr. H. - Acting Associate Dir. stating I would be submitting for Ruby Thomas to be upgraded from a GC III to a GC IV on 1/5/2007
- o Submitted the Executive Summary Package
- o E-Mail from J.A. - HRO, on 1/9/2007 stated that Mr. M. - Deputy Director, placed the reallocation on hold until further notice
- o E-mailed to C.H. - Administrative Aide, to check on status to see if the reallocation was still on hold
- o E-mail dated 5/14/2007 from C.H., stated Mr. H. still working on the reallocation
- o E-mailed to C.H. on 6/27/2007 checking on status again

- o E-mailed to C.H. again on 7/2/2007 checking on status
- o E-mail from J.A. HRO on 7/3/2007 stated not aware of any plan to upgrade
- o E-mailed to A.A-W - RC Supvr. on 8/21/2007 asking her to check on the status
- o 9/5/2007 e-mail from A.A-W stated T.'s -Clerk MI- position to be upgraded from MI to a III went to the VRB but no one had gotten back to her regarding Ruby Thomas' upgrade
- o 9/7/2007 A.A-W was told by HRO there was no packet on her
- o 9/10/2007 asked L.F. - Administrative Specialist II if he had paperwork for Ruby
- o 9/12/2007 asked L.F. again regarding paperwork
- o 9/12/2007 response from L.F. stating that he had strict orders to only work on an Annual Report
- o 9/20/2007 e-mailed A.A-W to check on paperwork for Ruby Thomas to see if C. A. Associate Director, ever received package from L.F. that I had recopied for the second time
- o 9/20/2007 the package went from L.F. to C.A. in meeting, there was a salary lapse that would have covered the upgrade for Ruby Thomas

REFERENCES F.
EMAILS TO INVESTIGATOR S.G. FROM RDT'S
SUPERVISOR - K.L. DURING EEOC'S
INVESTIGATION IN JULY 2010
EMAIL FROM K.L.L. DTD. JULY 07, 2010 RE: EEOC
COMPLAINT_(CONT'D)

o   11/1/2007 e-mailed A.A-W to check the status
o   11/2/2007 e-mail from C.H. stated that it was not being considered
o   11/5/2007 B.L. - HR Office requested that the package be resent to J.A. HR Officer to be reviewed and discussed with D.B. Deputy Director
o   11/5/2007 or shortly thereafter, A.A-W hand carried the package to LA.
o   Resubmitted request 4/23/2010 to have the PSA II that I now Supervise as well as the GC I/II upgraded to a General Clerk III and once again have Ruby Thomas upgraded from a GC III to a GC IV

From: J.R.A – HR Officer
Sent: Wednesday, July 07, 2010 2:51 PM
To: K.L.L. Administrative Asst.
Subject: RE: EEOC Complaint
K.
Thank you for the chronology of events. This is very helpful.
J. -HR Officer

Since my lawsuit was never heard in a court of law, and the opportunity to present my evidence before The Honorable Magistrate Judge was dismissed and Motion was allowed for Maryland County's Summary Judgement, No Justice was provided especially since the case was not presented before a jury/pretrial/trial.